SAINT PAUL

David Self

Illustrated by Jason Cockcroft

LION
CHILDREN'S

Saul Just Watched

IT ALL BEGAN in Jerusalem. There, Paul was known to everybody by the Jewish name Saul and he was a very clever student of the Jewish law.

Like his father, he was a Pharisee. The Pharisees were a Jewish group who spent much of their time studying God's laws – so Paul had left Tarsus (where he had worked as a tent maker) to study with them in Jerusalem.

A few years earlier, when Jesus was teaching and healing, the Pharisees had at first agreed with what Jesus was saying. When he became more and more popular, they turned against him – especially because some people began saying what all Christians now believe: that Jesus was not only a good man but also God's own Son.

In the end, the Pharisees helped to bring about the death of Jesus on a cross.

Jesus' closest followers, known as his disciples, believed he then came back to life and they started persuading more and more Jews to follow his teachings. They chose a number of these new followers to help look after any of them who were in need – such as children whose parents had died or widows who had no one to care for them. One of these helpers was a man called Stephen.

Stephen was a tall, energetic young man. He soon persuaded many Jews to become followers of Jesus.

The members of the Jewish Council, including some Pharisees, were

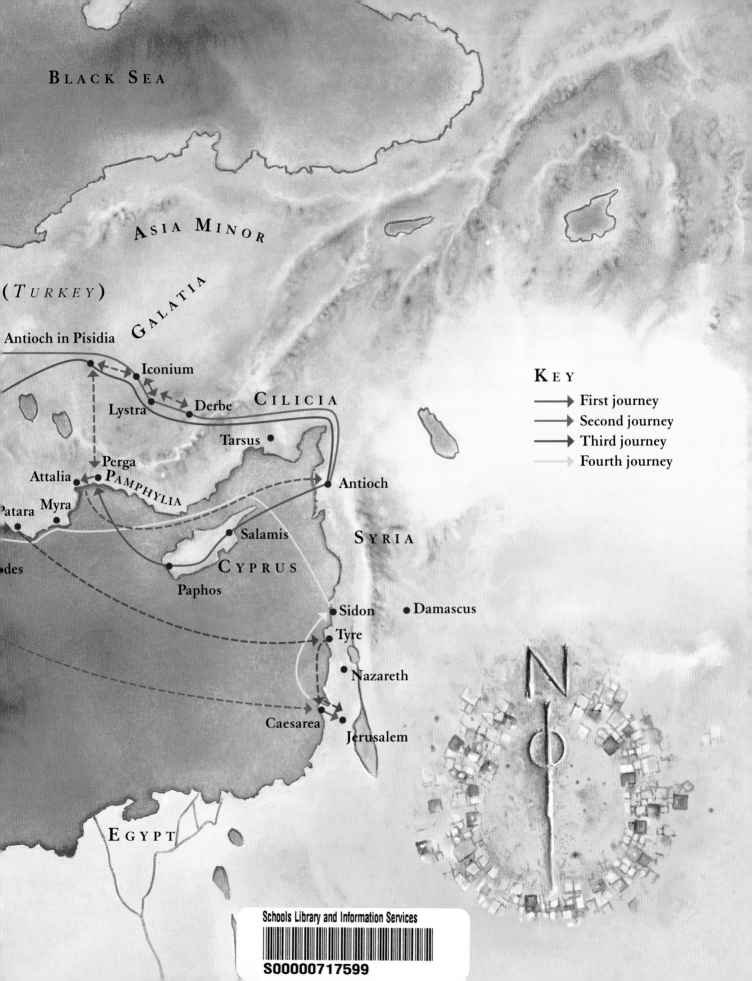

BLACK SEA

ASIA MINOR

(TURKEY)

GALATIA

Antioch in Pisidia

Iconium

CILICIA

Lystra   Derbe

Tarsus

Perga

Attalia   PAMPHYLIA

Patara   Myra

des

SYRIA

Salamis

Antioch

CYPRUS

Paphos

Sidon   • Damascus

Tyre

Nazareth

Caesarea

Jerusalem

EGYPT

KEY

→ First journey
→ Second journey
→ Third journey
⇢ Fourth journey

N

In memory of David, who died before
he could see this book finished.   M.J.

Text copyright © 2009 The Estate of David Self
Illustrations copyright © 2009 Jason Cockcroft
This edition copyright © 2009 Lion Hudson

The moral rights of the author and illustrator
have been asserted

A Lion Children's Book
an imprint of
Lion Hudson plc
Wilkinson House, Jordan Hill Road,
Oxford OX2 8DR, England
www.lionhudson.com
UK ISBN 978 0 7459 6097 5
US ISBN 978 0 8254 7906 9

First edition 2009
This printing January 2009
10 9 8 7 6 5 4 3 2 1 0

All rights reserved

Acknowledgments
The Bible retellings are based on the corresponding
passages in the *Good News Bible* and the *Holy Bible, New
International Version*; the scripture quotations are taken
from the *Holy Bible, New International Version*.
The *Good News Bible* is published by The Bible Societies/
HarperCollins Publishers Ltd, UK © American Bible
Society 1966, 1971, 1976, 1992.
The *Holy Bible, New International Version* is copyright
© 1973, 1978, 1984 International Bible Society. Used
by permission of Zondervan and Hodder & Stoughton
Limited. All rights reserved. The 'NIV' and 'New
International Version' trademarks are registered in
the United States Patent and Trademark Office by
International Bible Society. Use of either trademark
requires the permission of International Bible Society.
UK trademark number 1448790.

A catalogue record for this book is available
from the British Library

Typeset in 14/20 Elegant Garamond BT
Printed and bound in China by Printplus Ltd

Distributed by:
UK: Marston Book Services Ltd, PO Box 269, Abingdon,
Oxon OX14 4YN
USA: Trafalgar Square Publishing, 814 N Franklin Street,
Chicago, IL 60610
USA Christian Market: Kregel Publications, PO Box 2607,
Grand Rapids, MI 49501

worried by this. They thought that if everyone started following the teachings of Jesus, it could mean the end of the Jewish religion. But how could they stop men like Stephen? The answer was simple. With bribes.

They paid a number of men to say that followers of Jesus (including Stephen) had been speaking against God, and saying that the Jewish Temple should be torn down and the Jewish religion should change. The members of the council then had Stephen arrested and brought to trial in front of the whole council. He was accused of these invented crimes.

'You've heard the evidence against you,' they said. 'What have you got to say?'

Stephen began to defend himself. He spoke boldly about what he believed and how he respected the Jewish religion – but he ended by saying something that really infuriated the council.

'You're the wrongdoers. You betrayed and killed God's own Son, Jesus. You murdered him!'

The members of the council exploded with anger. They put their hands over their ears, trying not to hear any more. 'Blasphemy!' they shouted. 'Blasphemy!'

By blasphemy, they meant Stephen was saying something about God that was untrue – because, of course, they did not believe that Jesus was God's Son. The punishment for blasphemy was always the same: stoning to death.

They seized Stephen and dragged him along the streets and out through the city wall to a rocky place that was used whenever a stoning took place. The man known in Jerusalem as Saul had watched the trial and now went to see the stoning. The men who had falsely accused Stephen took off their cloaks so they could throw heavy rocks and stones at Stephen more easily. They gave them to Saul to look after. Then they started stoning Stephen.

Stephen knelt down and prayed as the stones began to hit him. 'Lord Jesus, receive my spirit into heaven and do not hold my death against these men.' More and more stones hit Stephen – on the head and on his body.

Even when he was close to death, Stephen was still praying for his executioners – but they kept on throwing until they were sure he was dead.

Paul, known as Saul, watched all this. 'It needed doing,' he said.

The stoning of Stephen had made up his mind. These followers of Jesus Christ were dangerous. They must be destroyed, wherever they were.

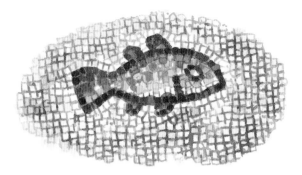

The Road to Damascus

THE VERY DAY Stephen was stoned to death, Paul started going from house to house in Jerusalem, determined to search out anyone who believed in Jesus. When he found any believers, men or women, he dragged them out of their homes and had them thrown into prison.

Despite this, in all the towns and countryside around Jerusalem more and more people were becoming disciples of Jesus. In particular, news reached Jerusalem that there was a large number of them in a city called Damascus, away to the north.

Paul went to the high priest of the Jews in Jerusalem and asked for official letters that he could take with him to Damascus. These letters would explain who he was and give him the power to seek out any followers of Jesus Christ, arrest them and bring them back to Jerusalem for trial.

Along with some other travellers, Paul set off on the long journey north, along the valley of the River Jordan, round Lake Galilee and across some mountains to Damascus.

All went well until they were near the city.

Suddenly, lightning seemed to flash all around Paul. He fell to the ground – and everyone heard a voice, addressing him by his Jewish name.

'Saul, Saul! Why do you persecute me?' said the voice.

'Who are you?' Paul asked, terrified.

'I am Jesus,' he heard the voice say. 'I am Jesus whom you persecute. Now get up and go to Damascus. When you get there, you'll be told what to do.'

The men who were with Paul were amazed. They had heard the voice but had seen no one. Paul staggered to his feet and looked around. It was only then he realized he could see nothing. He was now blind.

One of the other men in the group took him by the hand and led him carefully the rest of the way to Damascus.

The Conversion of Paul

DAMASCUS WAS ONE of the oldest cities in the world, and it was surrounded by high walls to protect it from any army that might want to attack it.

The men who were with Paul led him into the city through the west gate. This gateway in the walls opened onto the main street that led right through the middle of the city. It was called Straight Street. They led Paul along it, past the open air theatre where the Romans organized entertainments and past what had been a royal palace but was now the home of the Roman governor of the city.

Further along the street, they found a house where people could stay.

It belonged to a man called Judas.

Paul stayed here three days. He was confused, frightened and unable to see. He had no idea what do – and for three days he refused to eat or drink.

One of the followers of Jesus in Damascus was a Jew called Ananias. He had a vision. God seemed to speak to him, telling him to go the

house of a man called Judas in Straight Street.
There, he was to ask for a man known as
Saul. This made Ananias anxious. He
had heard all about this man and
what he had let happen to Stephen
back in Jerusalem.

'Don't worry,' said the voice
of God to Ananias. 'He's been
praying. He's had a dream in
which a man called Ananias
comes to cure him of his
blindness.'

Ananias was still worried.
'But we've been warned. He's
come here with power from
the chief priests to arrest any
followers he finds.'

'I've chosen him,' said the
voice, 'to tell all people about me.'
So, nervously, Ananias did
as God had told him. He went to
Straight Street, found the house of
Judas and went in. 'God has sent me
to you, Saul,' he said. 'Jesus himself, who
appeared to you on the road here. He's sent me so that you might see
again and believe.' And he put his hands on Paul.

At that moment, Paul's sight returned. He was baptized with water as a sign that he too was now a disciple – and the first thing he did was have something to eat.

Next, without delay, he went out and began to preach all he knew about Jesus. He knew a lot because, of course, he had been going around saying it was all nonsense. But now he was saying that Jesus had spoken the truth. Paul was no longer condemning Jesus' followers but praising Jesus as the Son of God.

Paul got so excited about his new beliefs that he immediately set about trying to persuade people to believe what he was saying. He spoke so well that many more Jews in Damascus became followers of Jesus. Of course, this angered other Jews in the city. They decided the only thing to do to stop him was to kill him the moment he tried to leave the city. They started keeping watch, day and night, just by the city gates.

Luckily, Paul's new friends heard about the plot. They went to him and explained there was only one other way out of Damascus.

Over the city walls.

That night, some of the believers in Damascus got a big basket and tied it to a rope. They put Paul in the basket – and then lowered it in the darkness down the outside of the city wall. It was lucky he was only a small man!

And as soon as he was safely outside Damascus, he set off – back to Jerusalem.

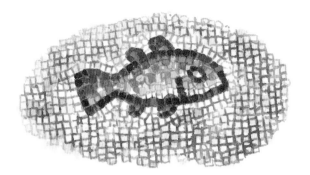

Not to Be Trusted?

AFTER HIS ESCAPE from Damascus, Paul hurried back to Jerusalem. He was still excited by what had happened to him and was bursting to tell everyone the news! He, Paul, had become a follower of Jesus Christ!

First, he rushed round to those who were already believers. 'I want to join you. I really do now believe you were right and that Jesus rose from the dead – and that all he said was true.'

These believers were suspicious. This man they knew as Saul seemed to be trying to trick them. After all, it was the man who had watched Stephen being stoned to death: Saul the Pharisee, who had had so many of their friends thrown into prison.

Paul tried to persuade them that he had changed his mind. 'I was wrong. I've seen the light of Jesus. On my way to Damascus.'

That wasn't enough. They were still afraid of what he might be up to.

But then one of them spoke up for Paul. This man was known as Barnabas. He too was a Jew but his home was far away on an island called Cyprus. He had come to Jerusalem when Jesus was teaching and preaching – and had become one of his closest followers.

Barnabas had heard exactly what had happened in Damascus. He explained to the other believers in Jerusalem how the man they knew as Saul could now be trusted – so they agreed he could join them.

Because he never wasted any time, Paul immediately started rushing round Jerusalem telling everyone he met the good news of Jesus.

Not surprisingly, this didn't please some of his original friends, the Pharisees. Some of them were so angry that they wanted to kill him. Once again, Paul's life was in danger. He didn't seem to be too bothered but the other followers of Jesus didn't want him taking any risks.

'It's time for you to go back home,' they said. 'To Tarsus.'

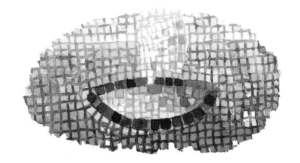

A Happy Meeting

So Paul went back to the city where he had grown up, Tarsus, in a district then known as Cilicia. There he was known by his Greek name, Paul.

'It's Paul!' said everyone. 'He's come home.'

Paul spent the next few years there but he wasn't idle.

That was never Paul's way. Half the time he was busy making tents. He had to earn a living, after all. The rest of the time he spent telling everyone he met about Jesus and what Jesus had taught about loving one another.

Then, one day, a stranger came to Tarsus. 'I'm looking for a man called Saul,' he said. Paul's friends went to find Paul. 'We think it must be you he's after,' they said.

Paul was suspicious. Were the Pharisees in Jerusalem still hunting him, angry that he had taken the side of the followers of Jesus?

'What does he look like?' asked Paul.

'He's a big, cheerful man – says his name's Barnabas.'

And so Paul and the man who had first trusted him back in Jerusalem met once again.

It was a happy meeting – even though Paul was very surprised to see him in Tarsus.

'Why have you come looking for me?' asked Paul.

'We need your help to tell people about Jesus.'

'In Jerusalem?'

'No. In Antioch,' replied Barnabas. Antioch was a city between Tarsus and Jerusalem.

Barnabas went on to explain how in Antioch those who followed the teachings of Jesus were now known as Christians – because Jesus was known as 'the Christ', which was Greek for 'the chosen one' or 'the special one'.

Barnabas also told Paul how it had been decided that you didn't have to be a Jew to become a Christian. It was something for everyone who truly believed in Jesus Christ.

Paul and Barnabas went to Antioch and spent a year there, teaching and preaching. Then the leading Christians in the city decided it was time that the Christian message should be taken to other countries. They thought it was a job for Paul and Barnabas, partly because they spoke Greek.

Everyone prayed for them and blessed them. Then Paul and Barnabas set off on the first part of their journey – to Cyprus.

The Lame Man of Lystra

PAUL AND BARNABAS set sail for the island where Barnabas had been born and had grown up, Cyprus. They landed at a town called Salamis, where the Romans had built a huge theatre and, next door to it, an athletics arena known as a 'gymnasium' or 'gym'. Both were open to the sky and Paul stood for a moment, watching athletes training in the gymnasium.

They moved on to the Jewish synagogue to join in the sabbath worship. There they explained some of the teachings of Jesus and explained how he had that said that, through him, people could have life everlasting.

Paul and Barnabas made their way across the island, stopping at different towns to preach the same message that Jesus was 'the promised one', the one whom God had told his people would one day come to save them.

They then took another boat to the mainland of Asia Minor. In each town they visited, people listened to what they had to say. Both Jews and non-Jews became Christians.

But Paul and Barnabas also made enemies. This happened in a city called Iconium. Some Jews and other people there had heard what they were saying and accused them of blasphemy – just as the members of the Jewish Council in Jerusalem had once accused Stephen. When some of the people of Iconium got ready to stone Paul and Barnabas (just as

Stephen had been stoned in Jerusalem), they quickly escaped to another city not far away: a city called Lystra.

In Lystra, they met a man who had been lame since birth. He had never been able to walk. As he was listening to Paul, Paul turned to him and said, 'Stand up straight!' The man hesitated.

'Go on, on your own feet!' said Paul.

The man stood up – and took a step. He was walking! He had been healed! All the local people were amazed and thought that Paul and Barnabas must be gods. And because the people were Greek, they thought that Paul and Barnabas must be Greek gods. They started

calling big, cheerful Barnabas 'Zeus', whom they believed was the king of the Greek gods – and they decided Paul was Hermes, their messenger, perhaps because Paul was the one who did all the talking but also because Hermes was said to heal sick people.

'We must bring a bull to sacrifice in your honour,' the people said, excitedly.

'You'll do no such thing!' said Paul. 'We're not gods! That's ridiculous. We're humans, just like you. You mustn't worship us.'

When Barnabas had calmed the people down bit, Paul explained why they had come to Lystra.

'We're here to tell you the good news. There's only one God, the one true God who made the world and who loves you and cares for you. He gives you rain when you need it, he makes your crops grow, he gives you food and everything –'

But then Paul was interrupted. Not by the crowd of people who were excited by the healing, but by some of the enemies Paul had made in Iconium. They had found out where he had gone after his escape from their city – and they also knew what had happened in both Damascus and Jerusalem.

'He's not getting away this time!' they said, grim faced. They seized hold of Paul and dragged him outside the city to stone him to death.

'Now I know exactly what Stephen felt like,' thought Paul. 'I deserve this.'

The first stones that hit him knocked him to the ground. He lay there, bleeding.

The men who had been stoning him were happy they had put an end to his teaching and left him.

When it was safe, his Christian friends came to find his body.

Paul sat up and groaned.

'You're still alive!' they gasped.

He nodded. 'Just about.'

He screwed up his face in pain. After a moment, he spoke again.

'It was nothing. Nothing compared to what Jesus suffered on the cross for us all.'

'True, but we're still going to get you out of Lystra.'

And they did.

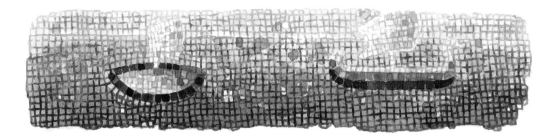

Off on His Travels – Again

PAUL HAD BEEN almost stoned to death in Lystra simply because of what he had said. Most people would be more careful what they said in future if something like that happened to them. Paul was different. He always said what he believed.

Because he was so determined to share his beliefs, he upset some people. And because he sometimes upset people, he got into trouble on many more occasions.

After their adventures in Lystra, Paul and Barnabas slowly made their way back to Antioch, the city they had set out from. They told all the Christians there about their adventures and how many of the people they had met had become Christians. Later, Paul visited Jerusalem – before going back to Antioch.

After a while, Paul and Barnabas talked about going back to the places they had visited on their first big journey. Barnabas wanted to take a young Christian called John Mark with them. In the end, Barnabas and John Mark journeyed to Barnabas's home on the island of Cyprus.

Paul chose a Christian from Jerusalem called Silas, who like Paul was both a Jew and a Roman citizen, to travel with him to visit the friends he had made in Asia Minor. After journeying through several towns, Paul turned to Silas.

'Now we're going to go to Lystra,' said Paul.

'Isn't that where they stoned you?'

'Yes.'

'And you still want to visit the place?'

'I've got good friends there.'

So that's where they went. In Lystra, they met a young Christian called Timothy, who had learned about Jesus and the Christian faith from his mother, Eunice, who was a Jew who had become a Christian, and from his grandmother, Lois.

'He's a good man,' said everyone. 'He'd be good to have with you.'

'Where shall we be going?' asked Timothy.

'I don't know,' said Paul.

'I see,' said Timothy, nervously.

'You'll get used to him,' said Silas.

'God will show us the way,' said Paul.

'Don't worry, Timothy. It'll turn out all right,' said Silas, never dreaming they would end up in prison – in a city called Philippi.

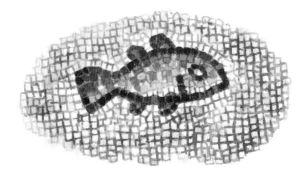

Purple Cloth Sold Here

LYDIA WAS A very rich woman. She lived in a city called Philippi which was just a few miles inland from the Mediterranean Sea. Philippi is in what is now called Greece but in those days was in a country called Macedonia – which (like most of the countries around the Mediterranean Sea) was then part of the Roman empire.

Lydia was rich was because she sold the very best purple cloth – and her customers were important Romans. Purple was the most expensive colour dye. Anyone could make red or blue or yellow dye. You could make cheap imitation purple cloth by dying blue cloth red. But the real, genuine purple dye was made only from a rare shellfish called the murex, which was found only in certain parts of the sea – and Lydia's fishermen knew exactly where to look.

Because it was so rare, cloth dyed with murex was expensive. Only the very rich could afford it: senators, emperors, people like that.

Every Saturday, the Jewish sabbath, Lydia joined the other Jewish people who had settled in the city of Philippi. They gathered by the river to pray and talk – and, as was usual in those times, the women sat a little apart from the men.

One particular Saturday, a group of strangers joined

them. Their leader was a little wiry man named Paul. The names of the other two were Silas and Timothy. There was also a Greek doctor called Luke. Later, Luke was to be the first person to write down the stories of Paul's adventures.

But Paul was the talker. The people of Philippi learned he had been a tent maker and was still well able to make a living from his trade.

At first Lydia wasn't inclined to pay much attention to him. But what he had to say was different to anything she'd heard before. She began listening more closely. He was talking about a man named Jesus, from the town of Nazareth. Lydia had never heard of Nazareth or of Jesus – but this man Jesus, Paul claimed, was actually God's Son, come to earth.

Lydia wasn't a fool. She was a clever businesswoman and she wasn't easily taken in. As she had so often said, 'You can't fool me. I know when a man's telling the truth.' But Paul convinced her he was telling the truth.

'You see,' she explained later, 'the more Paul told me about Jesus, the more I knew that I must follow the teachings of that man.'

Paul said the way to start was by being baptized, being lowered under the surface of a river. Lydia had heard of people being baptized but she had never fancied it! 'Being made an exhibition of, getting my best sabbath clothes soaking wet, there in the river for all to see, that's not my way. It would be embarrassing.'

That's what she thought at first. But Paul explained the point of being baptized. 'Being lowered under the water and then resurfacing, that's like dying and being born again. An old life ending and a new life beginning. All our wrongdoings can be washed away and we can start again, helped by the power of Jesus, knowing that his Holy Spirit will be with us.'

To the surprise of everyone, Lydia then asked to be baptized. Paul looked at her and said, 'If you believe with all your heart, you may be baptized.'

Lydia thought for a minute. 'Yes. I believe. I believe that Jesus is the Son of God.'

There and then, Paul led her down into the river and said, 'I baptize you in the name of God the Father, the Son and the Holy Spirit,' and he gently lowered her under the water.

Later, Lydia described how it felt. 'It was when I came up into the sunlight again that I really knew – knew God was with me and that I'd joined the friendship of all Christian believers.'

And there in Philippi, Lydia became the first known person in Macedonia to be baptized a Christian.

Prison – and an Earthquake

WHILE THEY WERE in Philippi, Paul and his friends met a slave girl in the street who was a fortune-teller. She thought a kind of spirit had got inside her and was telling her the future – and people paid to hear what she said. Because she was a slave, all the money she earned went to the men who owned her.

Paul didn't want to have his fortune told. Instead, he told her about Jesus. At once, she wanted to be a Christian and started running through the streets, shouting to everyone about Paul. To quieten her down (and because she still believed the spirit was in her), Paul told the spirit to leave her.

Her owners were furious. If she stopped telling fortunes, they wouldn't get any money. They seized Paul and Silas and dragged them off to the Roman rulers of the city. There they accused them of being foreign troublemakers and of causing riots. They never gave Paul or Silas a chance to say a word.

By now, a whole crowd was shouting insults against 'these foreigners' and saying they shouldn't be in the city. For peace and quiet, the city rulers took the side of the mob.

The city rulers ordered their soldiers to

give Paul and Silas
a savage whipping
and throw them into the
city prison. Silas didn't know
which was worse: the pain from the
whipping, not being able to move –
or fearing no one would ever rescue them.

Then Paul suggested they sang, so he and Silas
began singing Christian hymns – and Paul said his
prayers in a loud voice. The other prisoners fell silent
and began to listen. Even in prison, Paul wanted to share
the good news about Jesus.

Then, around midnight, there was a rumbling noise. It got louder and louder, and everything began to shake. Paul and Silas realized it was an earthquake. Even the walls began shake. It seemed as if the whole prison was going to fall on top of them.

After one particularly big shock, there was a crash – and not only did the gates of the prison cells break open, but the walls moved slightly and the chains round the prisoners' feet came loose.

Then the prison guard appeared – with his sword drawn.

But he wasn't about to kill the prisoners: he was about to kill himself. He was certain his prisoners must have escaped, Paul in particular, and that he'd lose his job and be put in prison himself.

Paul shouted out to him, 'Don't harm yourself. We're all still here.'

Someone brought a burning torch. The prison guard saw Paul and Silas and fell down at Paul's feet. 'How can I be saved?' he asked.

'Simple,' said Paul. 'Believe in Jesus. Then you'll be saved — you and all your family.' And Paul told him the whole story of Jesus and what he had taught. The guard listened. Then he took Paul and Silas to his house, bathed their wounds — and became a Christian.

Next morning, word went round the city that Paul and Silas hadn't tried to run away during the earthquake. Impressed, the city rulers sent soldiers to tell them they were free to go.

That was not good enough for Paul. 'Listen,' he said to the soldiers, 'they didn't give us a fair trial. We weren't found guilty, but you whipped us in public and threw us in prison. Now we're told to slip away quietly. We're Roman citizens.'

The soldiers scuttled back to the city rulers and told them Paul and Silas were Roman citizens. The rulers scurried round to the prison. 'Let us lead you out of prison ourselves to prove you are innocent and free to leave the city.'

And that's what happened. Except Paul and Silas didn't leave at once. They stayed at Lydia's house — and continued to tell the people of Philippi about Jesus.

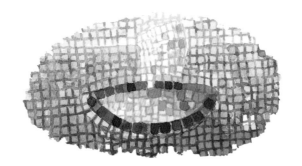

Cut-purse Corinthians

PAUL JOURNEYED ON alone to the busy sea port of Corinth. He'd heard enough about this city to be very careful. He went up to a rich merchant who looked as if he might be able to help.

'Can you tell me where the Jewish synagogue is?' he asked.

'I could,' said the man, 'but it'll cost you.'

'You mean I've got to pay you just to tell me the way?'

'You know what they say about Corinth? It doesn't fit everyone's pocket.'

'It's expensive then?' replied Paul.

'I'll tell you this for free,' said the man. 'Watch out for street thieves. They'll cut the purse from your belt. Corinthian cut-purses, they call them. They don't know right from wrong in this place.'

Paul stayed in the city for over a year with a man called Aquila and his wife Priscilla. They both were Jews who had become Christians. Like Paul, they earned their living by making tents – so Paul worked with them. After a while, Silas and Timothy joined him in Corinth.

Paul tried to preach Christianity to other Jews in the city but they didn't want to hear what he had to say and so he spent more time spreading the word to non-Jews. Many of them became Christians.

In the end, though, Paul decided it was time to return to Jerusalem. He never forgot his Christian friends in Corinth and later wrote them two long letters. In one of them, he remembered the athletes he had

seen, years before, on the island of Cyprus.

'Living a Christian life,' he wrote, 'is like running in a race. You have to train hard. Then you have to aim for the finishing line – and run as well as you can, as if you really want to win the race and gain the prize.'

In one of these letters, he reminded the Corinthian Christians about the importance of meeting together to follow Jesus' teaching that his followers should share bread and wine in memory of the Last Supper he had the night before he was crucified.

Paul returned to Jerusalem by way of Ephesus, a city in Asia Minor. Later, he made a third great journey with Luke through Asia Minor and to Greece, visiting old friends and taking the Christian message to new places. Then he returned once again to Jerusalem.

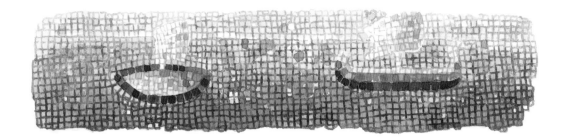

The Appeal to the Emperor

Back in Jerusalem, Paul was welcomed by all his Christian friends, who wanted to hear about the three great journeys he had made. It was different when he went to worship in the Jewish Temple. There, he had enemies who started whispering among themselves.

'That's the man we used to know as Saul!'

'He's the one who lets non-Jews worship in our synagogues.'

'Everywhere he goes, he persuades Jews to forget about Moses and the prophets.'

This wasn't true. Paul had kept true to the Jewish faith but also believed that Jesus had come to earth to save and help all people and not just Jews.

Within a few minutes, the whisperers had gathered together a crowd that became an angry mob. They seized Paul, dragged him out of the Temple and were trying to kill him. The commander of the Roman troops in the city heard the noise and quickly brought some officers and soldiers down to where the trouble was.

The commander couldn't work out what the row was about, but he arrested Paul to avoid his being killed. Even then, the soldiers had to carry Paul because the crowds were still trying to get near him and were shouting, 'Kill him, kill him.'

For two years, Paul was kept under arrest, partly for his own safety, partly because the local Roman governors didn't properly understand what the Jews were accusing him of. Finally, Paul demanded (as was his right as a Roman citizen) to be sent to Rome and tried before the emperor.

By then, the local governor, Festus, had decided Paul had done nothing that deserved imprisonment, never mind death, and had been prepared to set him free. But because Paul had demanded his right to be proved innocent in front of the emperor, he was sent by ship with some other prisoners to Rome. His friend Luke went with him.

Shipwreck

THERE WAS A strong wind blowing. The Mediterranean Sea was trough and the ship was making slow progress through the waves.

On it were Paul and other prisoners, all being taken to Rome. Also on board were soldiers to guard them, and Paul's friend Luke.

Eventually they reached the island of Crete. It was autumn so Paul suggested to the army officer and the captain of the ship that they stayed in a harbour there to shelter during the worst of the winter weather. 'To go on now will be dangerous,' he said.

The captain of the ship said no. 'There's a much better harbour further on.' They set sail again.

Soon a strong north-easterly wind got up. It was so violent that the sailors couldn't steer the ship and had to let it be buffeted along by the gale. The waves smashed down on the ship's decks and the ship began to sink. There was nothing for it: they had to throw some of the ship's equipment overboard to make the ship lighter.

There was so much spray that they saw neither the sun nor stars for several days, and the sailors and soldiers feared they would soon drown.

'I'll tell you something,' said Paul helpfully.

'What?'

'You should have listened to what I said.'

That didn't make him popular.

Then Paul told them all that he had had a dream that not one of them would lose their lives and he would reach Rome to stand trial.

For a fortnight, the ship was blown helplessly westwards by the storm.

Then, one daybreak, they saw land. They steered the ship towards a sandy bay but it stuck fast on a sandbank some way offshore. The pounding waves began to break it to pieces.

The sailors wanted to kill Paul and the other prisoners in case they swam ashore and escaped. But the officer in charge said no and ordered all those who could swim to swim ashore – which they did.

When the ship began to break up, the rest just clung onto planks or other broken pieces of the ship… and waited.

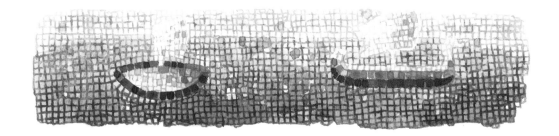

Snakes Alive

THE PEOPLE OF Malta had seen the ship driven by the gale towards their island. They had seen it stick on the sandbank. They had watched some of the men on board leap overboard and struggle to swim through the rough water towards the beach.

Then they had seen the ship break up under the pounding waves. Those still on board had clung onto bits of wood and been washed ashore by the waves.

The islanders rushed down to the beach and began to gather wood to make fires to help the survivors get warm and dry.

Everyone who had been on the ship was wet through – not just from being in the sea. It was now starting to rain as well. It was also a very cold day. The prisoners, the sailors and the soldiers were all shivering. But they were alive. They were safe. And so were Paul and Luke.

In fact, all 276 people on board reached the beach safely. Now they wanted to get warm and rest.

Paul was different. He began rushing around, helping the islanders gather up sticks. Just as the fire was getting hot and he was putting his sticks into the flames, a snake shot out to escape the heat. It sank its fangs into Paul's hand.

'This man must deserve death,' said one of the local people. 'He may have escaped from the shipwreck but now he's been poisoned.'

But Paul had already shaken the snake off his hand into the fire. Everyone watched, waiting for a wound to swell up or for Paul to drop down dead. He didn't. He just smiled. 'I'm all right.'

Paul and the others all stayed on the island of Malta for the rest of the winter. During that time Paul healed many sick people.

Three months later, still under guard, he was taken on another ship. It sailed up the coast of Italy, and then the soldiers took Paul by road to Rome – in chains like any ordinary prisoner.

House Arrest

IN ROME, PAUL was allowed to rent an ordinary house and live in it – except he was still under arrest, was kept in chains and had a Roman soldier to guard him.

Despite this, he was allowed visitors including Timothy and Luke – and many Jews also came to hear him teach. Once, Paul talked for a whole day about Jesus and what he had said and done. Some of the Jews living in Rome were convinced and became Christians. Other Jews thought that what he said was very wrong. At this time, many other people in Rome were turning against the Christians and many were put to death.

For two years, Paul lived under house arrest, welcoming everyone who came to see him – and writing letters to Christians in places he had visited on his earlier journeys.

He didn't actually write the letters himself. As he once admitted, his own handwriting wasn't very tidy, so he dictated them to a helper. He had so much he wanted to share that his ideas tumbled out of his mind in a great rush. Sometimes it took those who received the letters a bit of time to work out what he meant.

One of his helpers was called Onesimus, a name which means 'useful' – so Onesimus was both 'useful' by name and for what he did.

In fact, Onesimus had been a slave but had run away from his master to hide in Rome. There, he had met Paul and become a Christian. In the end, Paul decided he should be sent back to his owner, Philemon.

'He'll have me put to death for running away,' said Onesimus.

'He's a Christian, like us,' replied Paul.

'But he won't let me off!'

'As Christians, we should each forgive one another if we've got a grievance against one another. Forgive just as Jesus forgives us.'

'But I was his slave.'

'I'll write to him, asking him out of Christian love to receive you back, not as a slave but as a brother.'

'Me? Equal with him?'

'We're all equal in the sight of Jesus – and of God. That is the good news of Christianity.'

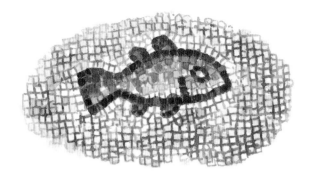

Memorable Words

No one knows for sure what happened to Paul in Rome. He may well have been executed during one of the times of persecution. He may have been allowed to travel – one of his dreams was to take the news about Jesus to Spain.

Whatever became of the man, his words have lasted and are treasured to this day.

If I speak in the tongues of men and of angels, but have not love, I am only a resounding gong or a clanging cymbal.

If I have the gift of prophecy and can fathom all mysteries and all knowledge, and if I have a faith that can move mountains, but have not love, I am nothing.

If I give all I possess to the poor and surrender my body to the flames, but have not love, I gain nothing.

Love is patient, love is kind. It does not envy, it does not boast, it is not proud. It is not rude, it is not self-seeking, it is not easily angered, it keeps no record of wrongs. Love does not delight in evil but rejoices with the truth. It always protects, always trusts, always hopes, always perseveres.

Love never fails. But where there are prophecies, they will cease; where there are tongues, they will be stilled; where there is knowledge, it will pass away. For we know in part and we prophesy in part, but when perfection comes, the imperfect disappears.

When I was a child, I talked like a child, I thought like a child, I reasoned like a child. When I became a man, I put childish ways behind me. Now we see but a poor reflection as in a mirror; then we shall see face to face. Now I know in part; then I shall know fully, even as I am fully known.

And now these three remain: faith, hope and love. But the greatest of these is love.

From Paul's first letter to the Corinthians

The Man Called Paul

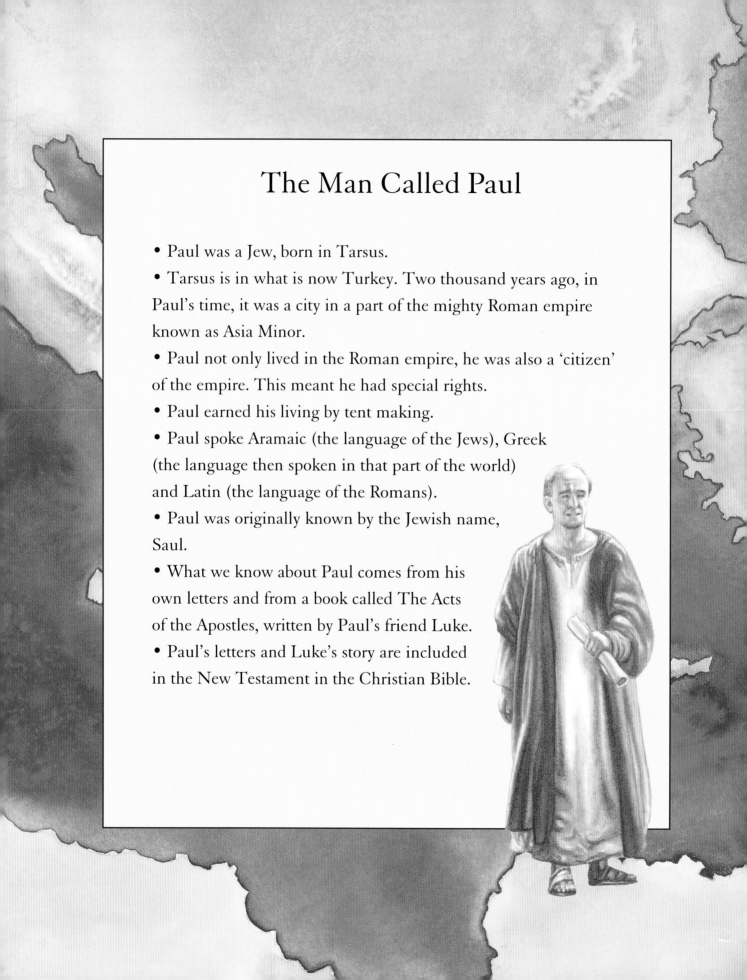

- Paul was a Jew, born in Tarsus.
- Tarsus is in what is now Turkey. Two thousand years ago, in Paul's time, it was a city in a part of the mighty Roman empire known as Asia Minor.
- Paul not only lived in the Roman empire, he was also a 'citizen' of the empire. This meant he had special rights.
- Paul earned his living by tent making.
- Paul spoke Aramaic (the language of the Jews), Greek (the language then spoken in that part of the world) and Latin (the language of the Romans).
- Paul was originally known by the Jewish name, Saul.
- What we know about Paul comes from his own letters and from a book called The Acts of the Apostles, written by Paul's friend Luke.
- Paul's letters and Luke's story are included in the New Testament in the Christian Bible.